Mary
Something-Else

Mary Hughes

Onwards and Upwards Publishers

Berkeley House, 11 Nightingale Crescent, Leatherhead,
Surrey, KT24 6PD.

www.onwardsandupwards.org

Printed in the UK.

ISBN:	978-1-907509-92-6
Typeface:	Sabon LT
Cover design:	Leah-Maarit

Scripture quotations from The Authorized (King James) Version. Rights in the Authorized Version in the United Kingdom are vested in the Crown. Reproduced by permission of the Crown's patentee, Cambridge University Press.

Endorsements

I first met Mary in 2003 at Herts International Church, Welwyn Garden City, where we both worship, and our mutual love for outreach and witnessing ignited a deep friendship and partnership in sharing the gospel with others. Mary's zeal and enthusiasm to share her love relationship with Jesus was highly evident from the outset, and it is interesting, after reading this book, to see what cultivated this passion.

In this transparent and simple autobiography, Mary takes us on a journey in which she is looking for 'something else'. Right from an early age she is consciously aware that there is a missing link in her life. The only problem is that she cannot identify or recognise it... until she is forty-five years of age – demonstrating that not everything can be microwaved.

Mary's life is miraculously transformed by the revelation of Jesus. She successfully presents her evidence without bias and without imposing her views on the Reader. In reading the book, I allowed myself to be a member of the jury. In so doing, I came to the conclusion that God was the intricate author of the story of our lives and orchestrates all our life movements, to allow us to discover our identity in Him – and He has not stopped. In the same way you, the reader, are invited to give your verdict...

Pastor Mandi Tandi
SFTN Leader, London Int. Church
Legal Trustee

This book is a wonderful testimony of Mary Hughes. A book which I found to be very interesting and which also reveals the love, grace and power of God in his redemptive role. I am particularly thrilled at how gently and lovingly God reached out to Mary; it reminded me of when Jesus Christ reached out to Saul who later bcame Paul. I was also thrilled how Mary recalled every detail of her upbringing and how God used her friends in fulfilling his plans for her life.

God uses people we can identify with to bring his purposes to pass in our lives, and we can absolutely trust him to bring our hearts' desires to pass because he is the "author and finisher" of our lives.

Well done, Mary 'Something-Else'!

Pastor Theodora Dare
Herts. Int. Church
Cert. in Christian Counselling
Higher diploma in ministries, LLM BL UK

I can't believe anyone would not find the answer to the question posed by so many ordinary people, after reading 'Mary Something-Else'. "I want something else" underlies the story of an ordinary lady leading an ordinary life with its ups and downs and tragedies. A ninety minute read leads you to the answer: JESUS. This is no ordinary testimony but an evangelist's tool. A must read for every person who wants 'something else'. After reading this book they are guaranteed to find it!

Alison Brown MA, PGCE, FRSA, MIAM
College Lecturer, Oaklands College, Herts.

This heart-warming biographical story will take you on a journey to find that 'something else' we all need. The author reminds us that external substitutes such as relationships, work or success cannot meet our deepest desires. That 'something else' we all crave is an authentic and loving relationship with our Creator!

'Mary Something-Else' is an easy, uplifting and inspiring read. It is a testimony that will leave you reflecting on your own journey with an assurance that God's plan for your life is always on course, whenever you sense it and whenever you don't.

Pastor Jacqueline Peart
Founder and Chair of 'Living in Wholeness', London
Jacqueline Peart Ministries

4

"Finally brethren,
whatsoever things are
true, honest, just, pure,
lovely, of good report, if
there be any virtue, and
if there be any praise,
think on these things."

- Philippians 4:8 -

About the Author

Mary Hughes née Swan, was born in Bristol, England in 1946. At the age of eighteen months, she and her older brother Ken emigrated with their parents to South Africa. They lived near Durban until Mary was five years old, then travelled up to Lusaka, in Northern Rhodesia (now Zambia, but then a British colony). After two trips back to England in 1956 and 1959, both for six months, Mary finally returned permanently to England with her parents when she was fifteen.

Married for thirty seven years, and now a widow, Mary lives in Welwyn Garden City, in Hertfordshire. She runs a small Bed and Breakfast in her home, and her daughter and four grandchildren live nearby.

Mary enjoys time with her family and friends, has regular trips to the cinema and theatre, and loves to go dancing and swimming. Having run her own business for many years, she now loves her 'freedom in retirement'. She keeps busy indulging in her pastimes of reading and following up her family tree, documenting all she finds in scrapbook albums. Mary's real passion, though, is for writing true stories taken from her own journey through life.

To contact the author, please write to:
mary.theark@hotmail.co.uk

Acknowledgements

My thanks to Sue Jackson for her patience and kindness in typing out all my handwritten words, also to Paul Langley for all his help – and hours! – spent on the technical side; so kind, Paul. Thanks also to Raymonde Fauchard-Newman for making me look 'my best' in the author's photo – such a good photographer you are. To you, and to all my friends at Herts International Church, including those who kindly took time to write their commendations, thank you so much.

I'm grateful to Luke Jeffery from Onwards and Upwards Publishers, who has been so patient with my technical struggles – it's so much easier with pen and paper – thanks Luke.

Thanks also to my brother Ken, who was able to 'fill in' the details of our trip from England out to Africa. He and I share so many happy memories of our years in Africa. He is my 'favourite' but only brother. Thanks, Ken, for your input. My memory only goes back to when we arrived at Umlaas Road in Natal, South Africa.

So many people have written encouraging words to me; each one served as a stepping stone to where I am now, about to embark on the second edition of my first book. I thank each and every one.

Most of all, thank you, my dear friend Polly, for your support and your enthusiasm. You have been such an encouragement to me, helping me every step of the way; you are a blessing, my sister-in-Christ, thank you — *xx*.

Mary Hughes

I dedicate this book to
my daughter, Jane, and
my four grandchildren,
Kenny, Catie, Molly,
and Hannah, *all* of
whom are my favourites!
(my most precious gifts)

Contents

Foreword by Dr Brad Norman

It is with great joy that I write the foreword to this short book, which is really a testimony of God's often undetected involvement in every detail of our lives, even the seemingly insignificant ones; that He works in tangible ways to weave the tapestry of our lives according to His design and that even things that we see as imperfect He incorporates into His perfect plan.

It has been such a privilege to have been part of one of the chapters of Mary's life; her story has blessed me and is now, I suppose, part of the story of my life too.

You will be encouraged as you read to see how you, as you learn to recognize and step into your 'God moments', can also experience such a relationship with a loving God, who calls himself 'Abba', your father.

Dr Brad Norman
Senior Pastor
Herts. Int. Church
Salvation for the Nations International Churches

Foreword by Pastor Andrew Reed

I have had the privilege of knowing Mary for a number of years, and throughout the book I see Mary's passion, humour and love for other people. I believe it is Mary's God-given love for others and her passion to see people come to know Jesus and grow in their relationship with Him that is her heart behind writing this autobiography. It is a testimony about her life, which is in essence a testimony of God's grace and evidence of His desire for all to come to know Him. With this in mind this book cannot fail to bless all those who read it.

Whether you are strong in your faith right now or finding things a little tough, whether you are currently having a hard time or everything in your life is good, whether you are young or maturing, whether you are in employment or at home taking care of the family, and whether you know Jesus as your Lord and Saviour or are just curious, this book will speak to you and enrich your life. You will be able to identify with so much of what Mary has been through in life and take comfort in how God always comes through.

Within this book Mary illustrates throughout her life, time and time again, God's faithfulness in answering prayer, giving us the desires of our hearts when those desires are best for us, and taking care of our needs as His children when we put ourselves in His safe hands and trust Him by doing what He says.

'Mary Something-Else' testifies to how God works all things for the good of those who love him. Even in the hardest of times, such as the loss of a loved one, God never leaves us and is always faithful. The story demonstrates how God brings people into our lives to bless us and so that we can bless them – some in a very obvious way and others more subtly.

I pray as you read this book you will be blessed on as many levels as I have been, whether it be concerning how God delivers and sets us free even from tough financial challenges, how He comforts us in times of trouble, or how He leads us through adventures in life.

In Mary's story we see an amazing journey of a wonderful lady who has fallen in love with Jesus, and the amazing life that has resulted; she is always looking forward to what God has in store next. It is amazing how God, through Mary, has positively impacted so many people.

I am looking forward to the next instalment because there always 'Something-Else' with God...

Pastor Andrew Reed
Herts. Int. Church
Salvation for the Nations International Churches

Introduction

I loved Africa. We all did. What an idyllic life we led: permanent sunshine, beautiful surroundings, living as we did in the 'Valley of a Thousand Hills'. Wonderful!

But from the age of two I became aware of a longing – for what? For *something else,* something more than I already had. Far too young to even begin to think what it could be, I would just whine to my mom, 'I want something else!' Usually with a pout – and possibly a stamping of my foot.

'Well, what do you want? A sweet?' Mom would ask.

Grabbing the opportunity, I'd reply, 'Yes! ... But I want something else!'

Mom would then offer, 'How about a cuddle?'

'Yes,' I'd say, 'but I want something else!'

After a while Mom would declare, 'Oh, I'm going to call you *Mary Something-Else* as that's what you're always asking for.'

I had a great childhood, spoiled rotten by my loving parents; I had lots of friends, toys to play with, animals to cuddle; what 'something else' was missing?

CHAPTER ONE

From Bristol to Africa

I was born on 16th October, 1946, in a three bedroom semi-detached house on the outskirts of Bristol, England – a third child to my mom and dad. Their first child, a boy, Thomas Charles, sadly died at just twelve days old – hospital neglect, my mom told me. My brother Ken was born three years later in 1941, five years before me.

My dad, a big, strong Englishman – red hair, ex-royal marine sergeant, ex-heavyweight boxer (very large broken nose!) – was so proud of his baby girl and doted on me for the rest of his life. He had a very Victorian outlook and was a proud, honourable man who, behind his tough image, had a very gentle nature; I loved him very much. My brother was always my hero, very accomplished in everything he turned his hand to – clever, talented and a great mimic and joke teller. We had a typical brother-sister relationship – lots of teasing, banter, and getting the wrong end of the rough and tumble. We speak once or twice a week to this day even though I now live in England and he in Canada.

What can I say about my mom? Well, if there is any such thing as a perfect mother, she was it: a tiny little Irish woman from Dublin (my dad at six foot towered over her five foot one frame); small feet and hands; an incredible sense of humour; and a total joy in everything she did. Being a mother to my brother and me was so fulfilling to her. When I picture her from my early childhood she is usually sitting at her Singer treadle sewing machine making dresses for me and miniature replicas for my dolls; or sometimes she is baking a cake or just washing her 'smalls'. She never knew how anyone could be unhappy with their hands in a bowl of warm, soapy water. (This was due to her memory of her poverty-stricken childhood with an alcoholic mother in Dublin; warm water was a luxury she did not often experience in those days.)

On Christmas Day, 1947, during the worst winter for fifty years, the pipes burst – putting out the flame on the Christmas Pudding! The water ran down the stairs, my dad rushed up into the loft to see what he could do and put his foot through the ceiling, and I screamed all morning in frustration because I couldn't manoeuvre my 'dog on wheels' bought as a present to help my walking.

As the plaster dust cascaded down into our already wet and freezing house (the only warmth coming from the kitchen or the fire in the lounge), my mother said, 'That's it! That's the last Christmas we spend in this country!' And by April 1948 we were on our way to a new life in South Africa. Needless to say, I don't

17

remember any of this part of my early eighteen months in England, but the family story has been told many times.

Mom and Dad were real pioneers to travel all the way to Africa with two small children in tow and no guarantee of a job or home at their destination. We arrived at Umlaas Rd, a little dot on the map about half an hour inland from Durban, in Natal.

Dad very soon started work in the local dairy, training to be a butter maker. Mom of course stayed home to look after me, while Ken was at school during the day. Life was great – and yet…

It was in Africa that I began to be aware of the longing for 'something else'. But at the age of about five or six I decided the 'something else' I wanted did not exist. How could it, if my mom did not know what it was? I experienced a sort of loss I couldn't explain, even to myself.

CHAPTER TWO

Lusaka

Dad was offered a job as manager of a dairy up in Lusaka, Northern Rhodesia, so we were on the move again: three days on the train up to this capital city of the British Colony, part of the federation of Northern and Southern Rhodesia and Nyasaland. I was then starting school so Mom travelled up with me the first day on the school bus. The Dominican Convent was situated six miles outside town, and so a new era of my life began. My 'something else' was pushed firmly into the back of my mind as I became embroiled in the religious rituals surrounding every part of every day. Mom, being an Irish Catholic, had brought me up in 'the faith' but I had never actually been aware of God until now.

I was fairly scared of the nuns – one Irish, one English and the rest of them German, all incredibly strict and with accents I wasn't used to. I was fairly bright so enjoyed all my lessons, but I always had this feeling of being trapped, and I longed for the day when

I could be free of school, free to do what I wanted. Mind you, at seven years old all I wanted to do was play and eat sweets!

I remember my catechism lessons, learning by rote set questions and answers like times tables – "One two is two. Two twos are four. Three twos are six..." Now the formula was:

> Q: 'Who made me?'
> A: 'God made me.'
> Q: 'Why did God make me?'
> A: 'To love him and serve him and be with him forever in the next world.[1]'

It was intensive training as we were coming up for our first Holy Communion, where I could dress up as a bride and be the centre of attention at Mass. Also there would be a celebration breakfast afterwards – a full English! – and a chance of receiving presents! But before communion there would be my first Confession.

Wait your turn in the pew. Go quietly into the confessional. Kneel, make the sign of the cross, and begin, 'Bless me Father for I have sinned; this is my first confession. I have been very cheeky to Mom and Dad. I told a lie. I am not very nice to some people.' And so on. (In later confessions this wording would change to, 'My last confession was so-many weeks ago.')

Soon after that you would leave the confessional (having had your sins forgiven by the priest) and kneel

---

[1] Or possibly '...for eternity.' I can't remember the exact words.

to do your penance – perhaps five 'Hail Mary's or three 'Glory Be's – dip your finger in holy water, make the sign of the cross, genuflect (a sort of curtsy) and then leave.

Now to Communion Day. I was very nervous, as we had been told how important it was to do everything correctly. Walk up to the front; kneel down, hands clasped in prayer, eyes closed. Lift head, open mouth, lay tongue on your bottom lip, and 'THE HOST' would be gently placed there. Take your tongue into your mouth, close your lips and (most important) *do not* bite or chew in any way; instead let THE HOST melt on your tongue, taking care not to get it stuck to the roof of your mouth, and then gently swallow. Rise and walk away from the altar with head bowed, and then back to your seat. Kneel and pray for a few moments, then sit quietly contemplating the enormity of what has just happened. (THE HOST was considered to be the transfigured actual body of Christ and not just a piece of rice paper.)

Well, I got it right, had a fuss made, a photo taken, a special breakfast and some presents! It meant nothing more than that to me. God was very much part of the grown up world of parents and teachers, always looking for me to misbehave so they could scold me in some way. I had no problem believing in God; I just didn't like him very much.

A few years after this, I went through a similar ritual of confirmation, which also had no meaning for me. Yet again, I passed 'with flying colours', Bishop's blessing, etc. What did it mean to me? Nothing other than an extra name to add to Mary Elizabeth. Now

Mary Something-Else

Joan of Arc was my chosen confirmation name. So I was now Mary Elizabeth Joan Swan – but I can't remember ever using the name Joan again.[2]

---

[2] It is interesting, however, that many years later I named my bed and breakfast business 'The Ark'.

CHAPTER THREE

School and General Life

I remained as a day scholar at the convent right up to the age of thirteen. We moved house five times during these years, always in Lusaka. The first move was out of our temporary dairy house to another, about a mile from the dairy. Dad would ride into work on his bicycle; I would still take the school bus. Our neighbours in this house were the Du Cladiers, a French family from Mauritius. The son, Henri, was Ken's age, and they became firm friends. The daughter, Danielle, was about three years older than me so I greatly admired her and hung around her often. We were friends until I was about ten or eleven years old.

I was with Danielle at school on an awful day, when I was falsely accused of stealing sweets. The nun told me that if I kept denying it she'd call a policeman and I'd be sent to jail! (I was six years old.) Thank God my mother believed me and came up to the school to tear a strip or two off the now-quaking-in-her-boots Irish nun. But I never felt vindicated, and the need to be perceived as an honest person has remained with me to this day. Danielle moved to a different school and we lost contact totally.[3]

From that house we moved out of town to a suburb called Emmasdale. Dad had lost his job in the dairy because after a whole year of riding to work at four in the morning on his bike (seven days a week) he finally saved up enough to buy a Morris Minor car and asked for a day off to take his family on a picnic to Kafue River. His request was refused, but he took us anyway (quite a rebellious act for my straight-laced father) and was promptly sacked, which meant we had one week to leave the house!

At Emmasdale we found a derelict house, which Mom soon turned into a boarding house. We lived there for three years before Dad joined the local British Government Offices, which made him part of the British forces, entitling him to Government housing and home leave every three years.

Our first home leave (England of course) was in 1956, four days by steam train to Cape Town, then two weeks on the Stirling Castle Ship to Tilbury Docks,

---

[3] Eventually, decades later, when I was in my late forties, I found her through my brother Ken's 'Lusaka News' (a monthly news-sheet for ex-Lusaka residents) and stayed three days with her at her lovely home in Durban. Her dad, in his eighties was now living in an attached 'Granny flat'. Forty years later, he still didn't speak English and seemed just as strict. But he couldn't remember me at all! Three days later, as I was about to leave, he came in and spoke in French to Danielle. She laughed and then explained, 'He just said he remembered you!' Apparently he said, 'Seven years old, plaits, freckles, no teeth; I remember her!'

London. We then spent six months visiting and staying with all our relatives whom I didn't know at all. Dad bought a beige Hillman Minx – straight from the showroom, I believe – in Canterbury. He shipped it back with us, and we drove back from Cape Town up to Lusaka – about three days' travel, staying in hotels on the way.

We were assigned another not-so-nice house on our return, a bit like a prefab. Mom was not happy with it as she couldn't hang curtains; it was fitted with venetian blinds. So she made a fuss and they moved us to another newer, smarter house. We stayed there until our next home leave in 1959.

All through these years, with the various house moves, I remained at the convent school as a day scholar. I suppose I was about nine when I started to cycle to school – six miles! No wonder I was such an athletic child – always on the go, full of energy. It was a blissful childhood, really – sunshine every day, parents who loved me, nothing to complain about... And yet, still I had the yearning inside. There were so many contradictions in the teaching of the nuns and priests; I always felt dissatisfaction and resentment. I saw injustice all around me and felt that I was not understood by anyone. I had the need to express deep emotions, boiling up inside me, but nobody to express them to. I really believed in God and knew he had made me – but what a vindictive God he must be, to make me such a troublesome child, full of cheek, too boisterous for my own good!

The nuns scolded me daily for being 'too loud' or 'bossy or 'cheeky' – the list went on. So why did God make me this way? At this rate it would be impossible to ever get to Heaven – it was so unfair! The people around me were unfair too, always misunderstanding me, thinking I was being cheeky when I was simply asking pertinent questions. How come all nuns and priests were guaranteed a front row seat in Heaven, while the rest of us had to earn our way there by doing good deeds, making sacrifices, and not doing anything considered enjoyable? Life was truly unfair!

Around this time, my mom was working for the Public Works Department (P.W.D.) and had made great friends with a work colleague, Wyn Tonge. Wyn had a daughter, Sandy, who was thirteen. I was twelve, so they introduced us, and she became the 'best friend' I'd been searching for all my life. We became inseparable – even rode to school together, parting at the last moment, as she attended the Jean Rennie School, not the convent. Sandy, an only child, and her parents, Wyn and Geoff, became my family's closest friends, and we all spent a lot of time together.

They were a completely un-churched family and viewed our churchgoing as slightly amusing. My dad had become a catholic convert when I was nine and was very fervent in his faith. My brother Ken, however, was totally bored with church, and he stopped going as soon as he was old enough. I knew just how he felt – church was *so* boring! But I was never brave enough to stop going; I believed that if I did that I would be destined for hell. All that fire and brimstone was to be avoided so I had to just stick to the church's rules and hope that God would one day allow me into Heaven. Not that I looked forward to that either, but it was certainly the best end of a bad deal. What was the point? To my mind, God had made me to enjoy all the things he didn't approve of and would not allow in Heaven.

There had to be something else worth living for, didn't there? What kind of God was he to condemn me – not just to an unfair life but to eternity doing good deeds, making sacrifices, not doing anything considered enjoyable? How could he be considered a loving God? I felt very alienated from him. Believe me, I tried on many occasions to voice my concerns, only to be met with shocked horror from the nuns that a 'good' catholic girl – where did that come from? – would even dare to ask questions that seemed to go against the teaching of the church! 'Put up and shut up' seemed to be the answer – so I did.

I remember feeling perplexed about some fairly basic teachings. For example, we were taught that the Pope was infallible; and yet, in History they taught us about the evil Borgias, one of whom was Pope – how did that tie in?

CHAPTER FOUR

A Big Change Ahead

In 1959 we were away again on our second home leave, this time on a different route: three days east to Mozambique; two days in Beira; then we set sail on a British India liner, the SS Kenya, for a five week cruise, up the east coast of Africa, Red Sea, Suez Canal, Mediterranean Sea, around the Bay of Biscay and on to Tilbury Docks. We stopped at twelve places en route, usually for a day but in Mombasa for four days. It was a fantastic trip.

We spent another six months in England; three months in a rented flat in Camberwell, in the middle of a cold winter; and three months visiting friends and relatives (including Christmas). Mom and I visited Dublin – a familiar place as we had visited there in 1956 – to spend time with her best friend whom she had rediscovered three years prior. During the week we spent there I met and fell in love with one of her six sons, Eddie, who was one of eleven children! I was thirteen, he sixteen. Love of my life, I thought at the time. But it would prove not to be...

The six months in England went quickly by, and during this time my father received a letter from his boss in Lusaka, informing him that on his return he was to be transferred to Fort Jameson. This place was three hundred miles out in the bush, a dot on the map – one shop, one golf club (of course!) and about one hundred white residents... but no school! So it was decided that I would continue in my convent school but now as a boarder – horror of horrors! However, there was no choice. At least before that we had the trip home to look forward to, this time on the SS Uganda, which was later used as a hospital ship during the Falklands War. Five weeks at sea, twelve places to stop at – and three days' train journey back from Beira to Lusaka.

By now I had had two six-month breaks – a whole year – of no schooling at all. But I returned with very high marks, and the only thing I never managed to catch up in was French. Apart from that, my schooling didn't suffer at all. However, if I had felt frustrated with school as a day scholar, I didn't have a clue as to how much I would hate school as a boarder.

I was under the control of nuns, who lived by strict rules: up at 6.30 a.m.; Mass most mornings; awful food; bed at 8.00 p.m.; lights out at 8.30 p.m. We had enforced study hours after school, back in our classrooms. I would spend the entire three month term in the school away from my parents, apart from three Sunday outings with Sandy and her parents between 11 a.m. and 5 p.m. and one long weekend with them from Friday to Monday. It was far from the freedom I had enjoyed before – riding my bike, visiting friends, going into town; all gone! There was no mention of boys, never mind mixing with them! The school was my prison: I couldn't leave the grounds; friends weren't allowed to visit; and all of our mail, incoming and outgoing (unless to or from our parents) was read, scrutinized and sometimes corrected by the nuns.

Thank God for my mother, who also found the Dominican Sisters just a little overbearing and 'over the top'. She was my ally. Mom would send Eddie's letters to me enclosed within her own letters. I would send my replies enclosed in my letters to her and Dad. She would also send instructions to the sisters at least once a term for them to take me to the dentist – and that was the only chance we had of a lift to town in the nuns' minibus, and a free hour for the appointment. Needless to say, I'd make sure my dentist knew I had 'no problem' with my teeth – a quick examination, occasionally a filling, then the rest of the hour to grab a hamburger and coke at 'Moggie's Milk Bar' in Cairo Road. Maybe I would even bump into some good-looking 'guys' and have a quick 'snog' before having to be back at the meeting place and back on the minibus with the nun!

If I had been caught 'snogging' (just kissing) it would have been punishable by expulsion. The same rule applied to smoking, which I never succumbed to – but other girls did and were duly punished. To be expelled was the greatest shame to be brought upon you and your parents; we were all so scared of these nuns.[4]

There were undoubtedly some very good women among our group of nuns, but unfortunately my life there seemed to be dominated by the few who were a very bad example and, I now recognise, a bad witness to the love of God. Apart from the very good friendships I made there, I hated boarding school.

---

[4] Years later, as an adult, I visited one of the sisters, now living in Germany, and was shocked to discover that even the younger sisters had lived in fear of the older ones – and also used to secretly smoke! Moreover, on a couple of occasions they had sneaked out of the grounds to visit parents living in a nearby suburb to have tea with them without the older sisters giving them permission!

CHAPTER FIVE

Faith and Questions

So, what to do about this belief but dislike of God? How was I going to deal with him for the rest of my life? I remember speaking to one of the 'nicer' sisters about it one day.

'So, if I obey the Ten Commandments and go to Mass every Sunday of my life, will I go to Heaven?'

She assured me I would. So there and then I made my 'bargain with God'. I remember saying, 'Okay, I can do that, one hour in church every Sunday, no lying, cheating, killing, stealing or coveting. That will keep me out of hell. Though I may not have a front seat in Heaven, at least I'll be there, which is the better of the two options.'

In the three years (almost) that I was a boarder, I spent the holidays with my parents in three different locations, as Dad was transferred two more times. The first three week break was in Fort Jameson, the next three of four breaks in Kitwe, up on the 'copperbelt', and the last in Livingston by Victoria Falls. Finally we returned to England for good in November 1962.

Would freedom from school give me that elusive 'something else'? Or would I get it from flirting with boys? Or from returning to England, seeing Eddie again, or marrying?

Eddie and I had stayed in touch by letter for the three years since we had met, declaring undying love and eventual marriage. We had both had other relationships during those three years but felt committed to each other nonetheless. After arriving in England, I spent a further week with him in Dublin and, later the same year, a week in England. However, I then finished my relationship with Eddie as I had met someone else. I still consider Eddie to have been my first true love. Our relationship had been passionate, with lots of kisses and hugs – but nothing more. We were much too young – and too scared!

The 'someone else' was my darling Pete, whom I'd met whilst working for Finefare supermarket in Hornchurch, in Essex. I'd only taken the job as a standby, whilst looking for an office position, so didn't expect to be there for long. Pete was a van delivery salesman for Wall's sausages and pies, and this supermarket was his first 'port of call' each day. He was known by all the staff as Pete Wall's, after his company name, as were all the other salesmen, e.g. Joe Lyons.

It was, if not love, then certainly a strong attraction on both sides. "As our eyes met over the sausage trays…" would become a family joke for years to come. It took several weeks for him to pluck up the courage to ask me out, and of course I said yes. He was very handsome, but, more importantly, he was gentle, kind, and could make me laugh, and soon we fell deeply in love.

We were both alarmed at our seven year age gap, our first date being weeks before my sixteenth birthday, whilst he had just celebrated his twenty third. However, we felt well suited, sharing the same sense of humour and many similar interests. Our choice of music was rock and roll. Our favourite group was Status Quo, and later also the Rolling Stones, and we saw both groups live on several occasions. There were trips to the seaside, meals out with friends, and of course the cinema, but nothing could compare to us just spending time together, wherever we were.

Pete had no religious background and referred to himself as 'either atheist or agnostic, can't be bothered to figure out which''. This wasn't a problem to me, however, as I felt it wasn't important. My Catholicism was 'set in stone' so we agreed to disagree on whether or not there was a God. My parents, too, were very happy with my choice; they really liked Pete, and perhaps felt he would be influenced by my faith. All I knew was that whatever his views, he was my dear, dear love.

Pete's father had committed suicide when Pete was just ten – a terrible tragedy. His mother had remarried a kind man who had become his stepfather. When Pete and I decided to marry in the Catholic Church, Pete's lack of faith became an issue. However, his mother then told him that his father had been an Irish Catholic, so he'd had Pete baptized as a baby. We managed to trace the baptism details so were able to marry officially in the Catholic Church, Pete promising to allow me to bring up any children we had as Catholic. He told me afterwards it meant nothing to him which faith I brought them up in as it was 'only one hour a week'!

We were blessed with a single child, our beloved daughter Jane – and what a blessing she truly is! 'Surely,' I thought, 'this beautiful baby girl, the most precious gift, has got to give me my 'something else'?' She certainly fulfilled a need in me and gave both of us deep happiness and contentment; my joy in her was overwhelming. But the gap remained – something missing that I still couldn't describe.

As in most marriages, we had our problems: lack of money and lots of illness. Pete was ill for several years. He vomited violently for days until he was sent to hospital. There he received anti-spasmodic injections, to be taken until his stomach calmed – but they couldn't find a cause. Jane was also pretty sick, and the doctors decided to keep this news from Pete in case his illness was psychological. It meant I had to shoulder all the responsibility – hiding Jane's tests that I had to do at home, pretending to him that there was nothing wrong with her so he wouldn't worry – an awful time, as I was 'worried sick' for both of them.

At the age of one, Jane was diagnosed with coeliac. This was a very rare condition in the 1970s, but at least I knew she would be fine on the correct diet. More importantly, I was able to tell Pete. Eventually he was found to have a duodenal ulcer, which required major surgery – in the nick of time as it happened – so he also recovered, thank God.

CHAPTER SIX

Work

When Jane was two years old I signed up to become a dealer for a well known plastics company, which was to become an obsession with me for the next twenty-four years! It alleviated the cash crisis, brought us many material benefits, and personally I found it incredibly exciting and satisfying. It also gave me the push I needed to take driving lessons as I was then 'given' a company car! Fantastic! Our lives changed drastically. I did so well at it that they offered me a distributorship after ten years, which involved us moving out to Hertfordshire from our West London home. More importantly it involved Pete, who gave in his notice at work, becoming my partner in the business. Jane was twelve so it was the perfect time to get her into a new senior school – Loreto College in St Albans. (Yes, like a good Catholic mother I had brought her up in 'the faith' so her junior and senior schools were both Catholic.) Pete still kept his distance from anything to do with Church, whilst I adopted a sort of pious, religious approach to my regular Mass attendance. I hoped my work would give me the 'something else'; but it didn't.

My mom sold her house down in Sussex. She'd been very lonely since my dad had died five years previously, so was only too pleased to join together with us and help us to buy a substantial house in Welwyn Garden City. It was an incredible blessing having her with us in her own little 'granny flat'. It meant she was there to babysit Jane during our long and difficult working hours. The house was beautiful and there were many material benefits to the job, but in fact it turned out to be very challenging for us both.

We had Mom with us for five lovely years until she died of a burst aortic aneurism at the age of seventy-seven. We were all devastated at her loss but were so pleased we'd been able to have her with us for those precious years. She left a huge hole in my life.

The challenging life Pete and I faced almost broke our marriage. However, we stuck with the job for fourteen more years (twenty-four in total for me). I thank God that Mom didn't witness the truly awful time in our marriage, the subsequent 'giving up' of our distributorship, and having to sell our beautiful house and move again, on the verge of bankruptcy. But in all this God's hand was still on us...

CHAPTER SEVEN

The Search

Over the years I had looked in many places for my 'something else'. Food was a strong contender, and I still have a weight problem as a legacy and reminder! Meanwhile Jane had given up all belief in God and for two or three years pretended to go to an earlier Mass just she could 'bunk off' it altogether. I discovered this years later. But in all that time I had never told anyone about my curious search – apart from my mother, and even she was unaware that I was *still* searching.

When we had returned to England in 1962 I had been filled with excitement. Firstly, I was leaving school ahead of everyone else. They had allowed me to take my exams privately before I left, and I had done very well. Secondly, I was excited at the travel opportunity – four days by train down to Cape Town, two weeks on the Transvaal Castle ship up to England – but also at the whole new adventure of starting again. It took several months for the horrifying truth to sink in – that

I might never see Africa again. I hadn't realized till then how much it meant to me.

There was very little I liked about England, and I pined for Africa so much. In fact, the only 'positive' in England had seemed to be the abundance of men. I went through several years of being very popular with the opposite sex, receiving wolf whistles and appreciative comments – and yes, I am not ashamed to say, I loved every minute of it! In those days, before feminism and political correctness, it was cool to be admired and treated like a desirable woman – though still totally innocent!

Within a year of being in England I had met and fallen for Pete – so life felt better – but it wasn't until we had married and moved to our little basement flat in Shepherd's Bush that I had begun to really appreciate living in London. The flat was dark, damp and dingy, but I had loved it. England had suddenly seemed far more interesting. Then three years later we had moved to Ealing W5. I had fallen pregnant and Jane had been born in September 1970. After that another twenty years had passed before I finally returned on holiday to Africa – twenty eight years after we'd left.

Then God really put his foot on my accelerator.

It was March 1990. As our plane began its descent into Johannesburg ('Jo'burg' as we called it) Airport, the clouds parted, and my eyes could see some trees and the red, red earth of my beautiful country, I burst into floods of tears, much to the embarrassment of Pete and Jane! What emotion it stirred in me! As we came through the gates, there waiting for us were Sandy and her mum, Wyn. I hadn't seen Sandy or heard her voice for twenty-four years, although she had visited me in England in spring 1966 and therefore had met Pete. We'd written constantly of course, but in those days international phone calls were rare and expensive.

We both sobbed in each other's arms – for about five minutes – then both said together, 'As I was saying...' as if we had never been apart. We spent a few lovely days with her, met her husband Nic and their five children – and loved them all. What a lovely family, and what a warm welcome they gave us!

Then it was time for us to go touring: a plane ride down to Cape Town; a couple of days there, then a hire car to drive along the garden route to Port Elizabeth; another plane trip from there to Durban; and another car hire drive up through Natal to spend the last few days with Sandy and family in Jo'burg. It was an emotional three weeks.

We stayed in some beautiful country hotels along the journey. Whilst in Durban we drove to Umlaas Road, half an hour inland, and managed to find the little hotel and two houses I'd lived in from the age of eighteen months to five years. I stood in the back garden of one of those houses and suddenly thought, for the first time in years, 'What *was* that something else? I never did find it.' However, I was still convinced that 'it' simply didn't exist – and put it out of my mind again.

But God was on my case.

On our return to Jo'burg, Sandy was preparing a big party for the twenty-first birthday of her oldest son, Jacques. He had decided that he wanted a whole sheep 'braaed' (barbequed), with all his friends celebrating with him. It was a great evening.

Jacques' friends asked us what England was like, as they had never been out of South Africa. One in particular, Vic, said that he intended to visit. So I invited him to stay with us, as Mom's granny flat had been vacant since she had died. Vic's own mother had died the previous year, and I remember thinking how sad it must be to lose your mum when you are just twenty-one. About a year later, in May 1991, he finally made the journey and came to stay with us as we'd offered.

CHAPTER EIGHT

The Answer

I had been looking forward to Vic's visit and had planned a whole 'mother substitute' role for myself. I wanted to fatten up this skinny kid and make a big fuss of him. But God had other plans.

As I opened my front door to him, the most extraordinary thing happened; I felt what can only be described as a flash of lightning between us. What was that? He didn't seem to notice anything, so I kept the smile on my face, invited him in, and showed him to his room. On and off, in between visits to Europe, he spent about five weeks with us. He was polite and helpful, no trouble at all, and yet... he really disturbed me. He followed me, always seeking me out, caring about my wellbeing and taking on a very fatherly approach, not allowing me to be a mother figure to him. I loved how he treated me but felt very nervous when he was around – dropping things, stuttering or tripping up!

I'd always felt confident and was a natural leader, yet this young boy was disturbing all of that. At one stage I wondered if I was attracted to him. The thought horrified me, as he was my daughter's age! I allowed myself to imagine the scenario of a romantic interlude – and, thank God, I realized this was not the case! I had no romantic inclinations towards him – but there was *something* there.

Vic was a Catholic (a charismatic Catholic, I was to discover later), and so he came to Mass with me every Sunday. But he went beyond my bargain with God in that he listened intently to the sermons – whilst I was just thinking about lunch! – and tried to discuss them with me afterwards. I just thought he was very odd for a young man; why would you want to talk about God outside of church? I was just a little embarrassed. He got on well with everyone, had a few outings with Jane and her new boyfriend Steve, but spent most of his time with me and, occasionally, with Pete.

One Sunday he and I were in Mass, and I was thinking about the fact that this was his last week with us – quite a relief really, as we'd be able to get back to normal. Without any warning, I burst into very loud, uncontrollable sobs – but I didn't know why. More startling still was Vic's reaction to this. Whilst everyone turned and stared at this sobbing middle-aged woman, he reached over for my hand, patted it reassuringly and said, 'I've been waiting for this. Don't worry; we have plenty of time.'

Well, that stopped my tears in their tracks! My first thought was, 'I have got myself a weirdo, probably a Moonie!'

As we came out of church I tried to take control by saying to him, 'Now, look, I don't know what is going on. All I know is, I don't want you to go and I don't know why.'

A silence followed, while he gazed at me in a sort of knowing way.

'Yes, I do...' I corrected myself. 'You have that *something else* that I've been looking for all my life – and you can't go until you tell me what it is.' It was like a slow recognition: all those weeks, this was what had been bothering me.

His next words amazed me. 'I know,' he said. 'Don't you remember what happened when you answered your front door to me when I first arrived?' But I'd said nothing at the time and assumed he'd not noticed anything. He continued, 'As I walked up your path, I asked God, "What am I really here for?" You opened the door and God said, "Her."'

That flash of lightning had been God's finger pointing at me. I had no problem believing in God, Jesus, the Holy Spirit, resurrection, etc. I had just never considered them to have anything to do with me.

What I'd been searching for all those years was, according to Vic, a relationship with Jesus. I argued for quite a while about my 'superior' knowledge of God and the Catholic Church, simply because of my age and wisdom. But by quietly pointing to Bible passages that explained what God was 'saying to me', Vic finally convinced me.

'Okay, Vic, you're probably right – but how does that help me? You've still got it, and I haven't.'

He smiled gently. 'That's easy! God wants a relationship with you, but he is a gentleman; he won't come in unless you ask him. That's all you have to do. Would you like me to take you through a little prayer?'

Yes, I would – so I repeated after him: 'I believe that you are Jesus, the Son of God, who lived and died for me and rose again. You are now seated at the right hand of God, where you live and rule forever more. I'm sorry that I haven't placed you as my Saviour and my Father, and for everything I have ever done wrong I ask your forgiveness. Please be the centre of my life. I commit all of my life to you. Father and Saviour, my friend and redeemer, please come into my life.'

This took place on August 1st, 1991. It was my new birthday – when I was *born again*. As I uttered the last few words from my heart, I felt, physically, a fist thump me in my chest.

'That's it!' I exclaimed. 'I have my *something else*. Jesus is my something else!'

At my invitation God's Holy Spirit now dwelt inside me, my body as his temple. I had never been surer of anything.

CHAPTER NINE

A Hidden Transformation

How do I describe all that has happened to me since? I have heard incredible stories of people who were completely transformed by their encounter with God: drug addicts who were instantly cured of their addictions; drunks who never touched a drink again; criminals who suddenly truly repented and made amends for all their crimes. The further they had fallen, the greater was their transformation. But my experience was less dramatic.

I could have described myself as a normal, middle class, average sinner, and very little change in me could be seen outwardly – at least, at the beginning. But inwardly I felt very different. The grass was greener, the sky bluer; I was filled with a deep satisfaction – and a surge of love that was astounding. I was suddenly aware of how precious my fellow human beings are. It's very easy to love family and friends, another thing altogether to feel love for strangers, particularly when they're dirty and smelly tramps, or physically unattractive, or just people you really don't like. I'd been incredibly selfish and self-centred all my life, so the love I now felt for all these people, whom I'd previously avoided, could only be God-given.

It's important to recognise that every encounter with God is unique to the person involved. Some people feel no different when they first come to know God but later become aware of a slow awakening of faith and a relationship with Jesus. Their encounter is in no way inferior to mine, just as mine is not inferior to the more dramatic encounters I have described. God loves us all and deals with us as we need to be dealt with – he knows best.

That first week I was filled with emotion – with love for Vic, who had allowed himself to be used as a vessel for God so that I could be born again. Vic was a great first tutor who, with endless patience, answered my many questions so wisely. But I was concerned that he was now leaving to return to South Africa. Vic explained that God would now guide me and would send more people to me; my learning was only just beginning. Meanwhile he would write to me as often as I needed him to. Vic's first letter to me was so full of love; he felt honoured to be used by God in such an awesome way.

I went to see my parish priest, an elderly man. Father Andrew was seventy-eight. I told him the whole story and let him read the letter. I was quite bothered by what I thought his reaction would be – but what a wise man he was!

First he asked me, 'How old is he?'

'Twenty-two,' I replied.

'No,' he said, 'he's one hundred and twenty two! He's an angel sent by God! You are blessed to have this relationship, and it's fine.'

I still have that lovely letter. I believe God used Vic to open my heart and my mind. For the next few months he and I corresponded regularly – Vic discipling me, drawing me closer to God.

I had a growing love and excitement for Jesus. How could I possibly have not liked him? Why had I never realized how wonderful, how loving, how marvellous our God is? But I didn't know what to do about it! I stood at the door of my open heart and mind, just gazing out in wonder.

I returned to Mass the following Sunday. I could hardly wait to get there – for the first time ever! I was a forty-five-year-old woman who had just fallen in love with Jesus. I wanted to cry and sing and worship my wonderful Saviour. I looked around at the congregation in frustration; why weren't they more enthusiastic? Did they not know they were in the very presence of Almighty God? Had I really been as unenthusiastic just one week ago?

Father Andrew retired soon after this and moved to Ireland. I was sad to see him go, but the door was open for another priest. Father Gerard joined us the following week, and I made sure I had a talk with him during the first few days. I repeated my story (my testimony) to him and was delighted at his response. He said he thought the Catholic Church – our local church, St Bonaventure, for instance – should do more to evangelize within its own neighbourhood. As he spoke I felt my heart leap – and I realized this was something I really wanted to do.

He announced his thoughts to the congregation and called together a meeting for anyone who felt called to do the same. About ten of us met the following Thursday to pray and discuss this. I was 'champing at the bit', longing to get out there and knock on doors to tell everyone about Jesus. Unfortunately it didn't happen quite that way. In the group there were only three of us, including Father Gerard, who felt like this. The other seven were very concerned about what we would actually say to people. 'Could we have a written script?' 'Do we target only Catholics?' 'Or should we target all Christians?' I felt they were missing the point.

They eventually agreed to go in twos to allocated streets and knock on doors and, when the occupant would answer the door, read from a script:

> Say, 'Good evening! Are there any Catholics living here?'
>
> If the answer is yes, continue, 'We represent St Bonaventure's Catholic Church, and we would like to leave a news-sheet with you listing all our services. You'd be very welcome to attend. God bless you! Thank you! Good night!'

Well, I thought this was bad enough, but it was even worse if the answer was no because then you would have to reply, 'So sorry to have troubled you!' And off you'd go!

Father Gerard was not too happy with the script. But he felt, as it was all they were willing to do, that it was worth letting them try it. I was so against it!

'First of all,' I explained to Father, 'I do not represent St Bonaventure's; I represent Jesus Christ. Second, I don't care two hoots if they are Catholic or not. In fact, *everyone* needs to hear about Jesus, particularly if they are not Christian.'

I did not want to use the script but instead wanted to allow myself to be prompted by the Holy Spirit. Father agreed with me and suggested that he and I could go out together; so on two or three occasions we did just that. It was wonderful! We would go out in the afternoon, choose a street, and knock on doors.

Father would begin, 'Good afternoon! I am Father Gerard and this is Mary. We are from St Bonaventures Church, and we are just in the area for anyone who would like to talk to us.'

Some of them were anxious to let us know that they weren't 'one of your lot'; in other words they were Church of England or Muslim, Hindu, Jew etc. But we assured them it made no difference; we were there for whoever needed us.

Others invited us in and offered us a cup of tea or coffee. These were always people in need or sick or recently bereaved. We would listen with sympathy and then Father would read a passage from the Bible, always appropriate for that person. Next he would ask me to pray. I realized I didn't have to say the traditional prayers but just speak directly to God – from my heart. What freedom! What joy!

Sadly, Father Gerard was moved on to 'pastures new' soon after, and I haven't seen him since.

CHAPTER TEN

Another Step

After six months passed we had more visitors from South Africa: Jacques and his friend Tony, whom I had also met whilst in Jo'Burg. Tony had been engaged to Leigh, Jacques' sister – but they were no longer in a relationship so Tony had decided to travel for a year and had brought Jacques with him. I felt disappointed that Vic wasn't with them; I so wanted to talk with him again.

I asked Jacques if Vic had told him what had happened during his visit to me. He said he only knew that we had shared some thoughts. I decided to tell Jacques all about it. When I had finished, Jacques said, 'That's so like Vic. He has helped so many people by being open to the Holy Spirit. I'd love to be used in the same way.' I realized then that he would be my 'number two angel' whom Vic had told me God would send.

I simply replied, 'You *will* be used, Jacques. You'll be my number two.'

He was ecstatic! 'Oh, wow!' he said. 'I was wondering who'd be my Bible partner in England!'

So began another chapter of my journey with God. While I was standing at the open door of my heart, wondering what to do next, Jacques pulled me through it. We studied the Bible together, he being a wonderful teacher, even though so young – just twenty two, but old and wise in his Christianity. He also took me to my first non-Catholic service – an evangelical 'happy clappy' type service (which I at first felt very embarrassed by). I looked around at all the people and felt such joy emanating from them. I was so moved by their love for our Lord and Saviour. I was aware for the first time of being part of these people, my brothers and sisters; we are all part of the body of Christ. I watched Jacques as he stood beside me talking to Jesus as if face to face. I was in awe and longed to do the same. But it would take me some time to be able to let go, raise my arms in the air and praise my Lord the way my heart and soul longed to do. First I had to get away from the religious spirit holding me back.

While all of this was going on, my poor husband was having a really hard time. As an atheist he had never interfered with my Catholicism, which he'd said only took an hour out of my week. But this was something different; this seemed to be taking over all of my life, and he didn't like it one bit. He objected to 'Bible bashers in my home'. By this he meant Jacques and I. He wouldn't let me play any Christian music and would rear up in anger at the slightest mention of anything Christian.

The night I got back from that first evangelical meeting (Mission For London with Morris Cerrulo) it was very late, and I expected Pete to be asleep in bed. The bed, however, was empty; Pete was not at home. I knew that he was angry, as he hadn't wanted me to go, and normally I would have been very worried – firstly that he would drive too fast in anger and have some sort of accident, but also in trepidation at the thought of dealing with that anger when he returned. About an hour later he came home, slamming doors as he came into the bedroom, ready for a row. But then the most amazing calm came over me, and I just lay with my eyes closed, not reacting or responding in any way to his anger. I just knew this was something he needed to go through, in what would be his own spiritual journey.

Eventually his anger subsided while I quietly prayed, and he fell asleep. Then, awake on my own, Pete fast asleep beside me, the most extraordinary feeling of joy swept through me, filling me as if through every cell of my body. It was an incredible feeling of love and acceptance, and release of everything that had held me back in the past – pure joy and happiness. I spoke to Jacques about it on the phone the following day, and he shrieked with excitement and threw the phone in the air. When he calmed down he told me that he felt I had experienced the baptism of the Holy Spirit. Wow!

When we next met, Jacques asked me if I was 'speaking in tongues' yet. I'd heard him and others use this amazing language that only God can understand, but actually I didn't feel this was something I wanted to do myself. As I explained to Jacques, I wouldn't feel it was genuine with me. I felt it was something that I could easily mimic and that would be deceitful. He said he would just pray about it. Over the next couple of weeks, whilst Jacques quietly prayed, it slowly began to dawn on me: my ability to mimic was a gift from the Holy Spirit, just as my ability to sing was a gift and not something accomplished by me. How arrogant of me to suppose that my 'speaking in tongues' would have anything to do with me. I know that every breath and every blink of my eyes depend entirely on the grace of God. I am nothing without him.

So, I opened my mouth, put my voice into action and let the language flow – and it did, in an amazingly liberating way. How can I explain what it is like? Imagine seeing the most beautiful newborn baby, or the cutest kitten or puppy. It's so gorgeous that you're overwhelmed with wanting to eat it! And you run out of words to describe how you feel. Well, when I begin to praise God and worship him, my love for him and recognition of his love for me cause me to run out of words – so I spill over to speaking to him in tongues. I have no idea what it is I am saying, but I am aware that my strange sounds are precisely expressing my love for my Lord. I feel a satisfaction inside, as if my spirit and soul are really connecting with God. He of course understands totally and fills me with his love. How did I ever live without being aware of that love?

Another change in me was this incredible love flowing through me for all people. Young or old, family or stranger, male or female, it made no difference. It's as if I can feel God's love for them. I have compassion for anyone who does not know the Lord. It's as if they are standing on the edge of a cliff about to fall off; I have to stop them! Of course my personality hasn't changed, in essence. I'm still a control freak; a bossy boots, some people say; very impatient; and generally fairly intolerant of other people's weaknesses. *But* I'm now acutely aware of my own failings. I'm learning lessons daily as God takes me from 'glory to glory', as he draws me ever closer. I'm amazed by his love for me, which I've never deserved, and the deep, deep certainty that I am his and he is mine, and that one day I will be with him in his loving arms for all eternity. Oh, the bliss of that certainty! Nothing matters in life compared to that.

One day, Jacques and I were in St Albans wandering around the market. We heard live music and followed the sound to the clock tower. A Christian rock group were performing on the street and handing out Bible tracts to passers-by. I was incredibly moved by these young people approaching complete strangers and speaking to them about God. I hoped I would be brave enough to do the same one day. The lead singer introduced himself to us. His name was Aiden. He and his wife Rosie invited us to attend a weekly Christian 'gig' called 'The Upper Room' – held in St Albans Boys School every Wednesday night at 8 p.m. We both attended that every week – and loved it! It was a youth group, but all ages were welcome, and I felt like I'd 'come home'. I attended this Wednesday night gig each week for the next few years and learned so much from these fabulous young Christians.

CHAPTER ELEVEN

From Glory to Glory

I attended an Alpha course[5] and loved it so much that I went back to four or five more courses, this time helping out. I so wanted to see people come to know the Lord that I prayed God would send people to me to hear the gospel. For two weeks he sent me a person every day. It was amazing!

For instance, I was demonstrating my company products in one lady's house over in Roehampton, in a very wealthy area. The elegant hostess greeted her guests very politely and made them all welcome. We had a lovely afternoon, and after all the guests had left we shared a cup of coffee before I was due to leave. From out of nowhere she began to share her innermost anxieties. I listened and sympathised, and then asked her if she knew the Lord. It was as if I had given water to someone who hadn't had anything to drink for

---

[5] Alpha courses seek to introduce the basics of the Christian faith, providing an opportunity to explore the meaning of life.

years. As I helped her to pray and she asked Jesus into her heart, I sensed her very real joy. I'll never forget what she said to me before I left. 'I feel as if I have a secret in my pocket that no-one knows about.'

I remember feeling the same way when Vic led me to the Lord. I wanted to hug the feeling to myself, but Vic chided me, saying, 'You have a bucket inside you that has been empty for so long. God is now filling it, and it is so wonderful that of course your natural instinct is to hold on to it for yourself. But once it's full you need to open the tap at the bottom and let it out to others; then you've got room left for God to fill you more and more.' That was just one of the many founts of wisdom – what an awesome man of God!

Although God sent one person to me every day during those two weeks, after that it stopped! I was so disappointed and spoke at length to Jacques about it. He said he felt that God had given me those fourteen people as an encouragement, but now I needed to take time to learn how to 'do it even better'. I needed to learn to talk about Jesus with God's steam rather than with my own strength and ability.

One day, Jacques' friend Tony was making the coffee while Jacques and I were studying the Bible. I said to Tony, 'You know, Tony, you are going to be my number three.'

He replied quite emphatically, 'No way! I don't believe what you guys believe. I'm not even sure I believe in God.' He was a lapsed Catholic.

But my prediction was correct. Within a year he and Jacques returned to South Africa, Tony joined Jacques' Pentecostal Church (only to help out by playing the guitar, you understand) and very soon after gave his life to God. A few months later, Tony's family moved to Spain, except his sister Anna who came to England to study nursing and lived with us for a while, before entering the nurse's accommodation at the QE2 hospital. Tony had led her to the Lord, and his whole family had left the Catholic Church and been baptized in the Mediterranean Sea. Tony's family, these lovely Portuguese South Africans, have now become a part of my extended family in Christ. I love them all dearly.

I can see such a startling pattern in God's plan for my life. He drew my mom and dad to journey to a new life in Africa. There he arranged for me to meet Sandy, who has been my dearest friend all these years.

Sandy was completely un-churched. Her first marriage ended when her husband passed away. Then, as a single mother to her three lovely children – Leigh, Linda and Bryan – she met and married Nic, who had two children – Jacques and Monya. Sandy loved him despite the fact that, much to her disgust, he was a 'Bible basher'. But God knew what he was doing, and it wasn't long before Sandy also gave her life to Jesus. The children then grew up in a Christian home.

Later, Jesus drew me back to Africa to meet Sandy's family for the first time and to meet Vic at Jacques' twenty-first birthday party. After Vic's subsequent visit to us in the UK, Jacques would then be used to further my 'journey into Jesus'.

Finally, Tony would become my 'number three', my wise counsellor, deeply Christian. But more to follow.

CHAPTER TWELVE

Evangelism

Evangelism is the gift God has given to me. I can't stop talking about my wonderful Jesus and have been used many times for his great purposes. Many people have given their lives to the Lord, and I can take no credit. But each time it happens I am more and more humbled by the tremendous privilege of taking people through the prayer of acceptance. I am so blessed.

During the first couple of years of my Christian life, I struggled with my Catholic upbringing. I still felt I belonged to the Catholic Church. That then changed to feeling that I *ought* to stay with the church in order to influence them.

Firstly, it was terribly arrogant of me to assume I was the only born again Catholic. I have since learned that there are many born again members – lovely, Spirit-filled Catholics, very devout and sincere, who are quite happy and fulfilled within the church. They are where God wants them to be, far more of a good influence than I could ever be. Secondly, as a baby

Christian I needed desperately to be fed spiritually. Much as I loved the Lord, I felt I was starving.

It was over two years after Father Gerard had retired before I finally decided to leave the Catholic Church and seek spiritual food somewhere else. The decision to make the change came through evangelizing a Jewish girl, who subsequently became a Christian. She was then desperate for me to take her to church. I felt led to take her to a Baptist church that I had heard was very lively. After one visit she was warmly received into their lovely congregation – and so was I. I was so drawn by the Holy Spirit there! I tried to split myself in two for the next few weeks. I'd go to the Catholic Mass, then rush off afterwards to join the Baptists at the tail end of their service. Vic came back to England on a visit and encouraged me to make the change and be properly fed by God on Sunday so that I would be more effective in my evangelism during the week.

So I left the Catholic Church with no guilt or regrets, and I became a member of the Baptist Church. There they offered me baptism, but as I'd been sprinkled as a baby in the Catholic Church, I didn't feel the need for it. They were very gracious and didn't put any pressure on me. But about a year later, as I attended another baptism, I suddenly thought, 'If it was good enough for Jesus, it's good enough for me!' – and I booked my baptism date.

What a fantastic experience! Mine was to be the only baptism on that day so a whole celebration was laid on for me, all the ladies of the church bringing food to serve afterwards to my family and friends who were to attend. I gave my testimony to all in attendance, and I was then fully submerged in the warmed-up water of the baptism pool, usually hidden under the floorboards of the stage. Even my husband Pete was there, at my daughter's insistence. I emerged from the waters as a new creation, my commitment to God public in front of many of my family members and friends.

At the time we had no permanent pastor. We were being looked after by the elders of the church. Members of the congregation were complaining that we really needed a pastor. I thought they were nuts! What was wrong with them? Could they not appreciate how wonderful our services were already? Why did we need a pastor? I had been used to turning up at a Catholic church over the years and occasionally being introduced to a new priest, as Father So-and-so had moved on to pastures and parishes new. But I was completely unprepared for what was about to take place.

We had a South African couple in our church who mentioned whilst on a visit home that there was a position for a pastor in their church back in England. Brad Norman felt moved by God to apply for that position. He and his wife, Wyona, came over to be interviewed by us, the congregation; we would decide whether or not to accept him. How extraordinary to discover that this was what was meant by a congregational church! The decision was not our only responsibility. We would also agree to provide him with accommodation, a car and wages, to support his wife and two teenage children. He would also require visits home to his sick mother in South Africa.

Brad made two or three visits to us over a six month period. On one occasion he preached at the service. Wow! Not a word about who was responsible for the church cleaning rota, or the flower arranging, or even the church fete or other fund raising events. No. Brad's preaching was directly from the Bible. It was like a banquet. I didn't want him to stop. The power of God reverberated through the church. This was what people had been waiting and longing for.

So Brad Norman became our pastor. As soon as I could, I arranged a meeting with him and told him my testimony. We 'hit it off' straight away, and he became my number four.

There is a pattern in God's plan here. All four of the 'boys' God sent to me were of the same age group (about twenty years younger than me), all of them were South African, three of them were directly connected to my best friend Sandy and Brad, and number four was from the same area I'd lived in when I was two years old and had first begun asking for my 'something else'. God is amazing! He brings everything together at the right time.

The news of Brad's preaching and the subsequent outpouring of the Holy Spirit soon spread, and people were drawn to our church. Within a year we had outgrown the building and couldn't fit people in. It was amazing! With reluctance, but led by God, Brad began to hold services in a local school hall and eventually in Oaklands College Hall in the centre of Welwyn Garden City. The majority of the congregation moved with him, but a small remnant from the original members remained at the old Baptist church and voted in a new pastor. Needless to say, I followed where God was leading me – with Brad and the newly established Herts International Church.

CHAPTER THIRTEEN

Kingdom Finance

Early on I had wondered how God would use me. I was so impatient to move forward and get on with whatever plan he had – but first I had to learn patience. I knew I had a heart for 'the lost' – those who have not received Jesus as Lord and Saviour. I wanted to be an evangelist like Billy Graham. I certainly had the gift of the gab and plenty of training in public speaking – but I was missing the point. *My* ability would have nothing to do with it.

> **Zechariah 4:6**
> *'Not by might nor by power but by my spirit,'*
> *sayeth the Lord of Hosts.*

I had, and still have, so much to learn of and from God. I struggled with the idea of prayer for so long. But eventually I realized it was simply talking to God, so now I talk to him all the time. I praise him and love him and thank him for all he is doing in my life. I trust him totally to supply all my needs.

Philippians 4:19
*And my God will meet all your needs according
to his glorious riches in Christ Jesus.*

I never worry about money, security, my future, or
how I'll get by; I just *know* that God is in control and
everything is fine. Praise God! He's never let me down.
Even when my finances have been in dire straits, with
no earthly solution, God alone has pulled me through.

For example, when my husband and I were
distributors for the plastics company, VAT was
introduced into the UK. A huge mistake was made by
the company, and distributors were wrongly advised on
payments to customs and excise. As a result all sixty-
two distributor couples ended up paying too much, and
we all ended up in terrible debt. Over fourteen years,
Pete and I overpaid by £240,000. If you multiply that
by sixty-two couples, you will see that the company
made a lot of money out of us! After many court cases,
well documented by the media, we were found to be in
the right – but unfortunately we were not allowed to
have the money back! Eventually we managed to
retrieve £32,000 on a technicality. It made no sense to
me then, and it doesn't now. Suffice to say we were all
in big trouble, and many couples lost everything – job,
house, car etc. Some cases were tragic: two people
suffered a nervous breakdown, marriages were affected,
and one person died from a heart attack brought on by
the extreme stress.

Pete and I pulled out of our company and were left
without jobs, with a huge mortgage and £240,000 of
debt. Interestingly, the debt was exactly the amount we
had been overcharged. Most of the debt was VAT and

was owed to Inland Revenue! But we still had to pay it! Other smaller amounts included a certain sum to the plastics company. We had no means to pay, and the first step seemed to be to sell our house.

Let me explain why I struggled so hard with this. When we had moved into this big house I'd always dreamed of, I had promised myself – as it was the twenty-first house I'd lived in – that it would be my last. I would design it to perfection, spend a lot of money doing so, and then would be content to spend the rest of my life in it. Although I must confess that a niggling thought at the back of my mind made me add, 'But if ever I had to move I would love that house on the corner!' My husband was not interested in my sentiment, however, and insisted that I would agree to put the house on the market.

One day I went out into my beautifully designed garden, looked around at what I considered my perfect home, and prayed to God. Finally I said, 'Okay, God, the house is yours, not mine. Do what you will. If I have to move, I know you will have something better for me.' Immediately a sense of peace washed over me. I walked back indoors and said to my husband, 'You're right. Let's put it on the market.'

Meanwhile, I had become aware that I needed to get my tithing back on track. Only a Christian can understand that when you need something you need to start by giving away.

Malachi 3:10-12
Bring the whole tithe into the storehouse that there may be food in my house. Test me in this says the Lord Almighty, and see if I will not

> *throw open the floodgates of heaven and pour*
> *out so much blessing that you will not have room*
> *enough for it.*

Well, my husband was a non-Christian so you can imagine how this idea went down. Like a lead balloon! He was furious and would not even discuss it. So I phoned a tithing ministry and asked them what I should do. They pointed out to me that my husband was the head of our household so I had to do as he said – *but* I could tithe personally in a very small way from my housekeeping. Every Monday morning I should tithe 10% of whatever was in my purse even if it was only 10p. They then prayed for me out loud on the phone that God would cancel my debts. I reported all of this to my husband, who scoffed at this 'stupid idea' but had no objection to my 10p or so tithe per week. So that's what I did. Within days we began to see our debts reduce.

The first time was in the dole office. To our shame we were claiming dole for the first time, even though it only lasted three months. I was told I owed them money because I hadn't revealed the small amount I had been earning in a new venture since leaving the plastics company. Well, of course, this wasn't true. I had revealed my small earnings, but they hadn't adjusted my dole money, so it was their fault. When they realized this they said something that made the hairs stand up on the back of my neck! 'We've never had a situation like this before. It is our fault so on this occasion we are going to cancel your debt.' Halleluia!

Next came a visit to the Inland Revenue who said, 'We've miscalculated your figures. You owe us £20,000 less than we first thought.' And so it went on! Our debt shrank from £240,000 to just £70,000 in just a few months. Praise God! Even my sceptical husband was impressed.

But we still needed to move. We searched everywhere for a house. We almost bought a lovely cottage, even paid £500 for the survey, but the sellers sold it to someone else. We had been gazumped! But as it turned out, it would have been far too small for us anyway. We eventually settled on another house, with another £500 survey. Neither of us liked it much but thought it would give us time to take a breather until we found the right place.

On the day we were to sign the contract, the most extraordinary thing happened. I answered a knock on our door, and there stood our estate agent who said, 'Mrs Hughes, I know you are about to sign the contract today, but I have to tell you that I have just found *your house*.' I went to see a house this morning to put it on the market, and as I stepped into it I thought, "This is Mrs Hughes' house. I don't know why!"'

I stared at him and said, 'It's that house on the corner, isn't it?'

He was astounded and asked, 'How did you know that?'

I said that I'd always loved that house but hadn't mentioned it to him when we were looking because there were two old ladies living there. They were two sisters in their seventies so I had been sure they weren't about to move – and even if one had died there would still be the other one.

But God had intended that house for us all along! We took one look inside and loved it. We were sorry to let down our intended sellers, but thankfully they very soon sold to someone else. And as for our two lots of £500 for surveys, our buyer offered us an extra £1000 to move quickly – so God gave us that as well! He is so wonderful. The reason the corner house was for sale was that one sister had to go into a home as she had Alzheimer's, and her sister loved her too much not to go with her. This house is where I now live. It is so much more *my home* than the big house ever was.

Finally, the new house cost £70,000 less than the big house so the difference cleared the debt. I hope that I will never have to move again – I'm so happy here – but I'll wait and see what God has planned for me!

I mentioned earlier that one of our debts was to the plastics company. We were outraged at this as it had been down to them that we had had any money problems. We refused to pay them anything, so for the next few years we had several threatening letters from their solicitors, which we ignored. We eventually got together with all the other distributors who were in a similar position. We determined to fight the company and hired our own barrister to do so. Eventually the company agreed to meet each separate couple to discuss settling out of court. They ended up admitting to 80% of the blame and only asking for 20% of the debt, yet another example of how our debts were reduced thanks to our wonderful God.

Incidentally, when the financial crisis took place I had been a Christian for about five years. It was interesting to see my fellow distributors' reaction to my conversion. I was so excited and full of the Holy Spirit. I was full on 'in your face' about my new found joy! People began to avoid me, saying, 'Keep away from Mary! She's got religion!' Yet I knew I was no longer religious but *free!*

> John 8:36
> *When Jesus sets you free – you will be free indeed.*

The Holy Spirit guided me to be more sensitive to where people are and not to force my beliefs on them. Some of these people who avoided me would later be drawn to Jesus in me, and he would use me greatly. Some of them have also now given their lives to the Lord. Halleluia!

CHAPTER FOURTEEN

A Turning Point

My early years as a Christian were wonderful, but they also caused a lot of heartache in my marriage. Pete really struggled to understand my joy in my newfound faith, and he couldn't accept it. He went through a lot of anger, and that slowly turned to jokey ridicule and eventually an amused acceptance that I'd religiously lost the plot and was to be humoured. I could cope with it and continued praying for him in the background.

At Christmas 2002, a remarkable change came over him for no apparent reason. We had discovered that we would be on our own for Christmas Day. My son-in-law had decided he wanted to spend Christmas Day with his family in Dorset. We encouraged our daughter and grandchildren to agree with him as he had never asked before. My husband sensed that I was dreading it – being just the two of us on Christmas Day – as things had been so unpleasant between us for some time. He resolved there and then to make amends. He decided to give me a really good Christmas Day, and in so doing, he also had a really good day. It was the start of a really wonderful year for us. We rediscovered the joy we had had in each other at the very start of our marriage, thirty-seven years ago.

At his suggestion we booked a three week holiday in South Africa (March 2003) staying with my friend Sandy and her husband Nick in their new B&B establishment in Cape Town. We had an amazing holiday despite the fact that I spent the last week in a wheelchair, having fallen and torn the ligaments in my right foot! Nonetheless the first half of the year was filled with blessing after blessing.

From about July, Pete began to feel very tired. Then on September 2nd, his sixty-fourth birthday, he had jaundice and was hospitalized. Tests were taken and the results given to Pete already on the first day in hospital, but he would not let the doctors tell me or Jane. He wanted to do that himself.

For a week and a half I visited every day wanting to know the results of the tests. Pete kept fobbing me off with, 'Oh, they are having a problem doing the tests because my plumbing is back to front as a result of my ulcer operation twenty-five years ago.' Or, 'Oh, the doctor had to go to an emergency. He won't be in till tomorrow.' I believed him because I wanted to believe him. I didn't want to think the worst, but some part of me knew that something was up.

I asked Brad if he would visit Pete and pretend that he was on a hospital visit and saw Pete by chance. I warned him that he might not get a welcome response – but I was wrong. Pete told me that Brad had visited and that they had had a long chat about 'the man upstairs'.

Pete said he thought Brad was 'a nice bloke' – praise indeed! He also joked that Brad was floating six foot off the floor and had a halo! After nine days in hospital they allowed Pete home for the day. I remember picking him up from the hospital door and being shocked by his appearance. He looked like a dead man – it was horrible. He was so weak and ill all day, but the day was so precious – like a gift. We were close and loving.

Pete began to talk and said, 'You know, I think there could be something to this religion after all.' My spirit soared with expectation – I just knew that God was working in him – but at the same time I was filled with dread, worrying that I might lose him. What a conflict of emotion!

I took him back that evening. Over the next two days he deteriorated, so he finally allowed the doctors to tell me the bad news. The tests had revealed cancer of the gall bladder and liver, and there was nothing that the doctors could do; his illness was terminal and he would have only days to live. The doctor also told me that Pete had requested Brad to come and see him. And so that night, Wednesday 17th September, 2003, I heard Brad lead Pete in the prayer of acceptance. Pete was now a Christian. Halleluia!

On Saturday 20th September my darling Pete died, with me and Jane by his side. We were devastated and thought we would never recover from the grief. That was also the week that Brad established his new church H.I.C. (Herts. International Church). I will never forget the anniversary. I found strength in my grief in the knowledge that I would see Pete again – that he is waiting for me to join him in Heaven.

All the hospital staff were amazed by Pete's bravery. But I wasn't amazed; Pete was the bravest man I have ever known. Over all his years of illness I'd watched him just accept it. He'd get up and go to work saying, 'Staying in bed is not going to help' – an incredibly brave man.

After Pete died, Pastor Brad told me of the conversation they'd had when he visited him in hospital. Pete had said to Brad that God had spoken to him and had told Pete to get his life in order and to fix for good his relationship with his wife. Almighty God, the creator of the universe, loved Pete so much that he met him in his atheism. What greater love can there be?

CHAPTER FIFTEEN

Journey to The Ark

My life changed dramatically, naturally. Without Pete I was no longer one half of a couple; I was alone, single, a widow – all the titles I had never wanted for myself. But God is good and my life was good.

When we'd pulled out of the plastics company at the start of 1996 we had signed up as unemployed – a sobering and humiliating experience. Pete had managed to find work after three months. I had looked at numerous 'party plan' companies and within a couple of months had joined two of them.

'JUST' were a Swiss company dealing in herbal medicinal (yet luxurious) creams and oils. I loved the products and knew I'd have no problem selling them. So I booked some presentations, recruited a few consultants, and I was off again doing the same type of work I was used to.

I also became a consultant for 'Creative Memories', an American firm opening in the UK teaching people to preserve their memories – photos, memorabilia etc. – in photo-safe albums. It was professional scrapbooking and great fun. In both of these companies I was determined to keep things low key and not build the business the way I had with the plastics company. But before I knew where I was, I was running two separate teams, one in each company! As the products were unrelated there was no conflict of interest. One year I was taken on by 'JUST' as a regional manager, and another year as a regional manager for Creative Memories. In the end I had to make a choice and the albums won. I cut down my whole job with JUST, but continued placing orders with them, supplying all the customers I'd collected on the way. I then quickly reached the top position in Creative Memories UK. I became their first UK director and won a trip to their head office in Minnesota USA. Following that there were many other trips and prizes. I went to Paris (twice), Monaco, Salzburg and Rome – it was brilliant. But the best part of all of it was how both jobs were platforms for my evangelism. I was able to demonstrate the oils as being 'God's plants that he has placed on the earth as a healing for the nations'. And when I held Creative Memories classes I would bring everyone's attention to one page, which held a mini testimony of how I had become a Christian. On many occasions I was asked to explain and had many Spirit-filled discussions. On at least two occasions I led people to the Lord. Thank you, Jesus! At one such class I was talking to a group of Asian ladies who turned out to be Christian. One of them ran a Christian Gospel radio show on a Sunday afternoon at Ealing Hospital in West

London. I was invited to go along one Sunday and be her guest speaker for two hours – what a privilege!

My team of Creative Memories consultants grew to 668 in number. There were only 1200 in the UK so over half were in my team. I was travelling a lot to train my consultants – driving and even making flights across to Dublin and Northern Ireland. I wanted to step back from leadership of my team and just look after my customers, but I couldn't afford to give up the monthly overide cheque (commission from the sales of my team).

One Sunday, the sermon in church was all about Noah's ark, and I suddenly realized I needed to call my house The Ark. I didn't know why, but the feeling was so strong that I went home, designed a plaque to put on my front wall and contacted a potter to make it for me. I wanted my house to be a refuge – but for whom? Perhaps I'd become a counsellor... I'd wait for God to lead me.

A few Sundays passed, and then the sermon was about 'stepping out in faith'. I knew God was speaking to me so I went to the front and asked for prayer. I resolved there and then to give in my notice the following day, giving up leadership of the Creative Memories consultancy team within three months. It was a huge decision, but I just knew that God would replace the money I'd be giving up. I bumped into Peter, our church's Bible teacher from South Africa. I confirmed with him what I had just committed at the front. He then told me he was looking for someone to help him launch a new product from South Africa into the UK. Was this part of God's plan? I told him I wasn't prepared to be an agent but would be happy to recruit other agents.

One day, whilst delivering some products to a customer, she told me about her B&B business. I immediately knew that was what I wanted to do. I left her house and went to the library to sign on as a Welwyn Garden City landlady. For the first time I actually used 'The Ark' as part of my address, not realising that it would put me alphabetically near the top of the list.

The following day I took a booking for my first ever guest and the phone hasn't stopped ringing since. What a success – fully replacing the money I had given up from my lovely team! God is so gracious! I love my Ark B&B; the business suits me so well. I have made many lovely friends, and on average I have been able to share my testimony with one person each month. When I had a frozen shoulder, God sent a German lady to stay with me for eleven days. She was a physiotherapist and gave me one hour of treatment every day for eleven days, didn't charge me and sorted out my shoulder by the time she left. God is so good! Everyone he sends is with me for a reason. One young man, Matthew, became a good friend. In 2009, he married a lady called Karen and invited me to his wedding in Cornwall. I made a whole week's holiday of it and had an absolute ball!

Incidentally, I live on Parkway, a beautiful duel carriageway in the town centre. Recently I heard a rumour that the garden area within Parkway had been originally designed to the specifications of Noah's Ark! My Ark B&B is in its rightful home. Isn't God wonderful!

Epilogue

As I am writing this book, it has been a year of adventure for me. It has included trips to Dublin (twice), to Cornwall and Cyprus. God has done so much in me, but he still has so much more to do! I'm filled with love for others, with such a burden for the lost and with no fears or cares about my life. I'm happier than I have ever been. Jesus is on my mind day and night. I chat to him, love and worship him. Sometimes I rant and rave at him, but I always know he is there. I worry about nothing. I know God is bigger than any problem that may arise, and I totally trust him.

My future excites me! I have no fear of death, just a longing to spend eternity with my Lord and Saviour, once I have completed 'the race' he has set before me. I confess that I would be very cowardly if my death were to first cause me pain; I'm not brave at all! But I'm not *afraid* of death because I know what comes after it will be unimaginably wonderful and joyful. God has put a firm assurance in my heart that when the day comes that he calls me home, I'll go whooping and hollering with joy.

My faith is stronger than ever. Unfortunately the opposite has happened with my lovely daughter. A few years after my conversion Jane had begun attending the Alpha Course with me, and after a few weeks she too had become a Christian. There had been an immediate change in her. She had become calm, peaceful and settled. But she struggled to find her spiritual home, and when her beloved dad died something inside her just closed up. She became very disillusioned and didn't want to hear anything about God. I'm sad for her, but she has committed her life to Jesus and I know he won't let her go. She is less aggressive about it now so she has to go on her own journey, and God is with her every step of the way. Praise God! I just have to keep praying, get out of the way and leave her in God's capable hands. He is watching over my grandson, Kenny, too, my twin granddaughters, Catie and Molly, and now my fourth grandchild, little Hannah.

I have found what I was looking for, all those years ago. But when Kenny was just two years old he came into the lounge one day and whiningly said, 'I want something else...'

How about you?

Do you know the Lord? Have you accepted Jesus in your heart as Saviour? If you haven't then don't waste another second. This could be your last chance; it's as simple as that!

> **John 3:16**
> *For God so loved the world that he gave his only begotten son, that whosoever believes in him should not perish but have everlasting life.*

I urge you to get right with God. In the end, it's the only thing that matters. You may feel that maybe it's not for you. The fact is, whether you like it or not, God made you with an aching void inside you. It is a void that only God can fill – and fulfil.

Ask him into your life. God will meet you where you are. Rich or poor, drunk or sober, ready or not, one thing is for certain: he will meet you in the midst of your sin. Yes, I'm afraid so – we are all sinners! Even Mother Teresa could not earn her 'Heaven ticket' on her own works, as good as they were. We all get to Heaven by God's grace. None of us deserve it, but it is offered free to all. We just need to accept him as our Saviour.

Philippians 4:8
Finally brethren whatsoever things are true, honest, just, pure, lovely, whatsoever things are of good report, if there be any virtue, and if there be any praise, think on these things.

Proverbs 23:7
For as a man thinks in his heart, so is he.